MY FRIENDS ARE FIGHTING

KEEPING THE PEACE

You Choose the Ending

by Connie Colwell Miller • illustrated by Sofia Cardoso

T0018689

Do you ever wish you could change a story or choose a different ending?

IN THESE BOOKS, YOU CAN!

Read along and when you see this:

WHAT HAPPENS NEXT?

→ Skip to the page for that choice, and see what happens.

In this story, Jasmin's two best friends are fighting. Will she help keep the peace, or will she get caught in the middle? YOU make the choices!

Jasmin has two best friends—Manny and Elijah. Usually, the kids create fun dance videos together. But today, Manny and Elijah are fighting over who gets to make the next dance routine.

WHAT HAPPENS NEXT?

→ If Jasmin joins the fight, turn the page.
If Jasmin tries to make peace, turn to page 12. ←

"You made the routine last time!" yells Manny. "So? I'm the better dancer!" Elijah shouts back. "Let me settle this," Jasmin says.

WHAT HAPPENS NEXT?

→ If Jasmin sides with one of her friends, turn the page.
If Jasmin stops the argument, turn to page 16.←

Jasmin thinks. "Elijah is a better dancer, so he should get to make the routine," she says. "Ha!" Elijah shouts in Manny's face. "I told you!" Manny is angry and embarrassed.

WHAT HAPPENS NEXT?

→ If Jasmin continues to take Elijah's side, turn the page.
If Jasmin backs down, turn to page 20. ←

"Whatever," Manny mumbles. "I'm better than both of you at remembering routines."

Jasmin steps in again. "Actually," she says. "Elijah is good at that, too."

TURN THE PAGE →

Jasmin and Elijah watch as Manny walks away. Jasmin realizes she should not have taken sides. She hopes an apology will help Manny forgive her, and she wishes she had acted differently.

THE END

→ Go to page 23. ←

Jasmin listens to her friends argue. Then she speaks up. "This fight is silly," she says. "We are all a part of this group. You're fighting when we could be having fun."

Jasmin continues. "We need all three of us to make our videos. And we're ALL talented. Let's stop arguing."

TURN THE PAGE →

Manny speaks up first. "Okay," he says. "I'll stop if Elijah stops." Elijah nods.

"Good. Then let's record our next dance video," she says. Jasmin is proud that she helped her friends make up.

THE END

→ Go to page 23. ←

Jasmin almost chooses a friend to side with. But she stops to think how that will make each boy feel.

"Manny, you're better at some things, and Elijah is better at others," Jasmin finally says. "Can we agree on that?"

TURN THE PAGE →

The boys look at each other. Jasmin can
see they are still mad. But they both nod.

After some cool-off time, the friends
start creating a new dance routine. Jasmin
is glad she didn't choose a side and make the
fight between her friends worse.

→ Go to page 23. ←

Jasmin sees she has hurt Manny. She realizes she should not have picked sides.

"I'm sorry, Manny," she says. "You're a great dancer, and we need you on our team."

But Manny says nothing.

TURN THE PAGE →

Finally, Manny speaks up. "I don't feel like dancing anymore today," he says.

Jasmin wishes she hadn't picked sides. Then everyone could have had fun making dance videos.

THE END

THINK AGAIN

- What happened at the end of the path you chose?
- Did you like that ending?
- Go back to page 3. Read the story again and pick different choices. How did the story change?

We all can choose how we act when people we love are fighting. If your friends were in a fight, would YOU choose sides, or would you help them work it out?

For our friends at the Yellow House with love.—C.C.M.

AMICUS ILLUSTRATED is published by Amicus
P.O. Box 227, Mankato, MN 56002
www.amicuspublishing.us

© 2023 Amicus. International copyright reserved in all countries. No part of this book may be reproduced in any form without written permission from the publisher.

Library of Congress Cataloging-in-Publication Data
Names: Miller, Connie Colwell, 1976- author. | Cardoso, Sofia (Illustrator), illustrator.
Title: My friends are fighting : keeping the peace : you choose the ending / by Connie Colwell Miller ; illustrated by Sofia Cardoso.
Description: Mankato, MN : Amicus, [2023] | Series: Making good choices | Audience: Ages 6-9 | Audience: Grades 2-3 | Summary: "In this choose-your-own-ending picture book, Jasmin and her friends try to make a dance video. When her friends argue, will Jasmin help make peace? Or will she make their fight worse? Readers make choices for Jasmin, with each story path leading to different outcomes. Includes four endings and discussion questions."— Provided by publisher.
Identifiers: LCCN 2021056821 (print) | LCCN 2021056822 (ebook) | ISBN 9781645492764 (hardcover) | ISBN 9781681528007 (paperback) | ISBN 9781645493648 (ebook)
Subjects: LCSH: Interpersonal conflict in children--Juvenile literature. | Friendship in children--Juvenile literature.
Classification: LCC BF723.I645 M548 2023 (print) | LCC BF723.I645 (ebook) | DDC 158.2/5083--dc23/eng/20211217
LC record available at https://lccn.loc.gov/2021056821
LC ebook record available at https://lccn.loc.gov/2021056822

Editor: Rebecca Glaser
Series Designer: Kathleen Petelinsek
Book Designer: Catherine Berthiaume

ABOUT THE AUTHOR

Connie Colwell Miller is a writer, editor, and instructor who lives in Le Sueur, Minnesota, with her four children. She has written over 100 books for young children. She likes to tell stories to her kids to teach them important life lessons.

ABOUT THE ILLUSTRATOR

Sofia Cardoso is a Portuguese children's book illustrator, designer, and foodie, whose passion for illustration goes all the way back to her childhood years. Using a mix of both traditional and digital methods, she now spends her days creating whimsical illustrations, full of color and young characters that aim to inspire joy and creativity in both kids and kids at heart.